# Making a Difference

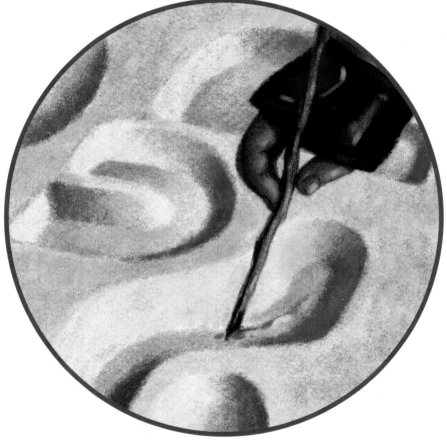

Patricia Almada
Illustrated by Mike Reed

Rigby®

Henry loved the cool breeze rushing past him as he skated. His shiny new wheels were the quickest wheels around. Henry flew through town. His skates were the wings on his feet.

It was a beautiful day and Henry couldn't wait to meet his friends at the park.

Henry arrived at the library and joined his friends Alex, Alicia, and Mark. Before they started to skate, the librarian came out and said, "Not here! You know the rules!"

"But there's room to skate here,"
said Henry.

"Rules are rules, even if there's
space," the librarian responded.

The kids chanted,

*"Not here, not there,*

*We can't skate anywhere!"*

And they skated away.

Soon they were at the park. They started to skate down a small path when the park keeper shouted, "No skating here!"

"But it's early, and no one is here," Henry moaned.

"Rules are rules, even if no one is here," said the park keeper.

The kids chanted,

"Not *here,* not *there,*

We can't skate anywhere!"

Henry, Alicia, and Alex took a seat at a nearby bench and wondered what they could do. When they noticed Mark drawing a picture in the sand, they went over to take a look.

8

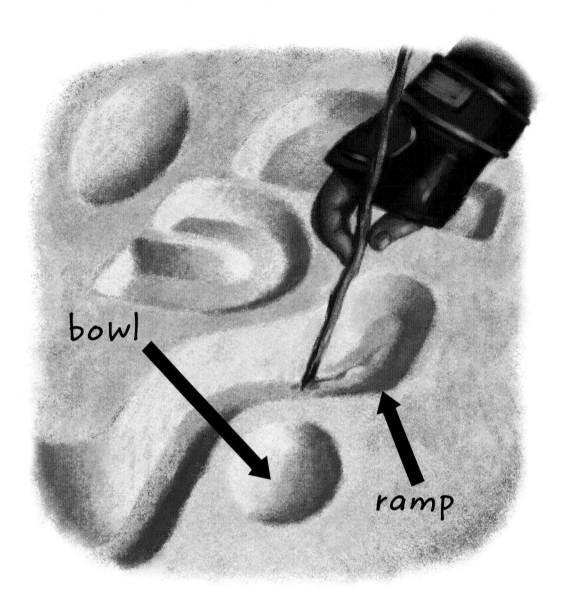

bowl

ramp

"The skate park where I used to live looked like this," Mark said.

"Wow, that looks amazing. I wish we had a skate park here!" said Alicia.

That evening Henry told his parents, "We need a skate park." He showed them his list of the problems the children were having and ideas he had for a solution.

| Problem | Solution |
|---|---|
| • no place to skate | • find a safe place to skate |
| • we could get hurt | • ask for help |
| • we are bothering people | |

"You can ask the city to build a skate park. Write a speech and present it to the city council," said Mom.

"Don't forget to include good reasons for your ideas," said Dad.

A week later, Henry, his parents, and friends went to the city council meeting.

When his name was called, Henry felt uncertain about whether he had the courage to share his idea. He walked slowly to the podium and read his speech.

Ms.Polynisse  Mr. Ellis  Ms. Sanchez  Mr. Hooper  Ms. Koo

City Council Members:

   I am Henry Parsico. I can't find a place to skate in our city. My friends and I don't want to bother neighbors or break any rules. Please help us by building a skate park so we can skate safely.

Thank you!

"Thank you, Henry. We like to hear from kids because they are important citizens," said the mayor.

Ms. Polynisse

Mr. Ellis

Ms. Sanchez

"The city council will discuss it and see if we can help. You'll have to be patient. These things take time."

Everyone clapped as Henry walked out. A reporter took his picture and promised to write a story about him. Henry felt wonderful!

"I'm proud of you," said Mom, "You were brave and responsible."

Henry's friends chanted,
"In our city, in our town,
We'll have the best skate
park around!"

# You Can Make a Difference!

If you want to change something in your community, you will need to be prepared, be ready to listen, and have patience.

**Step 1:**

Talk to your friends and brainstorm possible solutions. You will also need the help of responsible adults, so discuss it with your parents or teachers.

**Step 2:**

Next talk to someone at City Hall. Look for the right person in your city's list of commissions, or ask for a city council member. They will be happy to listen and give you advice.

## GOVERNMENT OFFICES

| | |
|---|---|
| Billing Information | 555-0412 |
| City Hall | 555-1000 |
| Emergency Services and Disaster | 555-1234 |
| Public Works | 555-5100 |
| Parks and Recreation Department— | |
| Recreation Office | 555-1586 |
| Building and Zoning | 555-7150 |
| City Clerk | 555-0812 |
| City Administrator | 555-3122 |
| Fire Department | |
| Emergency | 911 |
| Non-Emergency | 555-6803 |

You may be asked to present your idea to a commission or city council. It may take time and compromise, but if your idea is good, the council might do it.

It's kids like you who make a difference in their communities. You can be a hero, too. You can make a difference!